JESUS
OUR
BROTHER
IN
SUFFERING

MESSAGES
FOR LENT
AND EASTER

JESUS OUR BROTHER IN SUFFERING

DENNIS A. ANDERSON

AUGSBURG PUBLISHING HOUSE
MINNEAPOLIS, MINNESOTA

JESUS OUR BROTHER IN SUFFERING

Contents

Contents

Preface

Kathy was 18 years plus. Kathy was dying of cancer. During the months that I called on her she never volunteered a complaint, in spite of the fact that pain reached such heights she could not walk. Kathy had to crawl across the floor in order to move from room to room. As is the case many times, it was the pastor who was inspired after the visitation perhaps more than the patient. I'll never forget the last call I made on Kathy. It was near the end of Holy Week. Kathy had been thinking about the nails in Christ's hands and feet. She had been meditating on the suffering of Jesus. When I entered her room she had a most pleasant smile on her face. She reached out her hand to take mine. "It's neat, pastor, really neat!" Kathy quietly whispered.

"What's neat?" I asked.

"The nails. When I think of the nails in Jesus'

hands and feet, it doesn't hurt so much any more. It's neat."

Pain and suffering are not always redemptive. Not all suffering has a benevolent outcome. We dare not "suffer" under any pseudo-pious preacher's delusions that there is something great about suffering. Suffering is never sought, even by the most serious and committed Christian. Anyone who plays easy with any kind of suffering, physical, mental, spiritual, or even suffering "for the sake of" Christ has not looked at the cross very deeply. Like Peter, we are not equipped to welcome suffering.

Yet, by the miracle of God's grace, suffering does become redemptive for some. Kathy was brought not only closer to Christ, but because of Christ's suffering, hers no longer seemed quite so bad. In fact, from her testimony her suffering became a bond with Christ. I pray, that should I ever meet such suffering, regardless of the cause, the results would be such for me.

As Christians we commit ourselves to remove the cause of suffering where we can. But its cause is not always known. The source of evil remains problematic. Scripture does not spend as much time dealing with cause as with the pragmatic need to "bear under," which is the literal meaning of suffering, and the announcement of God's ultimate overcoming.

Bonhoeffer says, "Suffering is to be cut off from

God, yet within the fellowship of Christ's suffering, suffering is overcome by suffering and becomes a new way to communion with God." Kathy discovered such a communion with Christ in suffering. For some of us, I am sure, suffering becomes a curse or is a curse which shows how cut off we are from God, or worse yet, how we have cut God out of our lives. Yet, here is Christ who "did not count equality with God a thing to be grasped, but emptied himself, taking the form of a servant, being born in the likeness of men. And being found in human form he humbled himself and became obedient unto death, even death on a cross. Therefore, God has highly exalted him and bestowed on him the name which is above every name . . ." (Phil. 2:5:ff.). Kathy found Christ her brother in suffering and as she found him to be her brother she discovered him to be her Savior. "It's neat pastor, really neat."

It is difficult for the preacher to preach on suffering unless he has experienced it himself. I resisted preparation of these sermons and preferred to let those who have "lived through" the various situations do the speaking. In a number of cases I sought the voice of those who have walked or are walking through the valley of the shadow and know that their brother Jesus is walking with them.

These sermons were written and delivered with the realization that those who come to worship during midweek Lenten services are *hungering* for what I would call "meat and potatoes." The congregation was challenged to "work" with me in thinking through the meaning of suffering and our relationship to the suffering of Jesus on the cross.

If these sermons raise more questions than they answer, they will have served a useful purpose in removing the tendencies toward easy answers in the face of suffering. Hopefully they will also help us to be more receptive to Jesus, our brother on the cross.

The series was written out of the following biblical and theological framework:

A. Scripture and church history display a progression of understandings about suffering and its causes.

B. Suffering is a result of an Evil One, yet God can turn some suffering toward positive results. Suffering under evil is not because God is out of control. Suffering produces three results:

- focuses attention on the suffering universe in need of redemption;

- draws people out of their idolatrous self-love;

- emphasizes God's sacrificial love as shown by our brother Jesus on the cross.

C. Old Testament Views on Effects of Suffering:

- There must be a hidden wisdom of God which causes or allows our suffering.

- There will come the "Day of the Lord" when all righteousness will be done. The evil will be punished and the good vindicated.

- Suffering calls people back from idolatry.

- Righteous suffering may at times absorb the sins of the guilty.

D. Jesus Christ on the cross adds a new understanding to suffering. Jesus does not assume suffering is good in and of itself. It becomes good because he willingly takes it upon himself "for the sake of others." "While we were yet sinners he died for us" (Rom. 5).

E. Christ suffers *with* us because of evil. He suffers *for* us to redeem us from evil. He calls us to come and suffer with him.

F. A God who did not abandon his own Son on the cross of suffering will not abandon his other children in their suffering. God is present in the suffering of the world and calls us to "take up the cross."

G. Christ does not call us simply to "accept" suffering. At times we are to protest against that which may bring suffering on us. But we are called to accept those who suffer, and help whenever possible. This is to bear his cross.

Two excellent texts which deal with the theme of these sermons are recommended to those who wish to read further are *The Crucified God* by Jürgen Moltmann, and *Suffering* by Dorothy Soelle.

I would like to express my appreciation to Alice Bett and Helen Mader for their loving and devoted help in preparing this manuscript.

Dennis A. Anderson

LENTEN

MID-WEEK

SERMONS

When I'm Hurt by the Sin of the World

"Oh, there's always
Someone playing Job."

(Archibald MacLeish, *J.B.*)

We gather here in this place of worship. We focus on the beauty of the altar, set for Ash Wednesday communion. Just blocks away several people lie in the hospital suffering from cancer. In place of wine in the chalice, the scene is dextrose dripping through plastic tubes into veins, keeping bodies alive. People suffer diseases that are at times senseless. There seems to be no cause, rhyme, or reason for some dread tragedies to strike.

In 1976 we saw the news photo of thousands who died and hundreds of thousands of others made homeless in a horrible earthquake in Guatemala. In May 1970, a devastating earthquake struck in Peru destroying a city and burying an estimated seventy thousand people.

The sands of the Sahara desert are moving inexplicably southward as much as twenty-five miles a year, drastically changing the climatic and farming conditions and bringing famine to more than 1.7 million Ethiopians.

Each day, the world we live in becomes more aware of its fragile existence and of the urgent problems confronting society. Tragic pictures depict the reality of suffering caused by starvation, population pressures, and human injustice.

Yes, there is always someone playing Job. By "playing Job" I mean someone who is suffering a tragedy brought on not by his own stupidity or sin, nor even by the evil of others. Tonight we struggle with the issue of suffering that seems to make no sense—suffering simply because there is evil in the world. St. Paul well describes the world when he says, "We know that the whole creation has been groaning in travail together until now, not only the creation but we ourselves. . . ."

Paul describes a world out of harmony, out of sorts, with itself and God. At times it does seem as if the world itself, not just its inhabitants, but the whole creation, is out of joint. Suffering because of the world's disharmony is the kind of pain of which we speak tonight. In Genesis 3:17 we are reminded that when people sin, not only are they out of joint with God, but with the whole creation. The ground itself and their own bodies both bear the consequences of the fall, the curse. "The whole world is in the power of the evil one" (1 John 5:19). Not only does each person need to be saved, but creation itself needs to be brought into harmony with God. "For God so loved the world that he gave his only begotten Son. . . ."

The Response of Avoidance

We try to avoid painful experiences. One evening I was watching a powerful but very painful film on television. At each commercial break I was tempted to switch channels because I did not want to watch the suffering. I was not suffering, yet I did not even want to be exposed to the suffering on television. In a survey, movie-goers said in effect, "We want more happy endings."

The avoidance of pain is a most natural human reaction in the face of suffering. We will go to extreme lengths to avoid facing the reality of pain and suffering. But in our day, the suffering of earthquake victims in another country, or of cancer patients locally can be brought into our homes. We can see their faces. It is no longer seventy thousand who are buried. We see their bodies exhumed. It is no longer a nameless and faceless child who is napalmed. We see his face burn. The cancer patient is no longer a statistic on the chart. We see him die. Via modern communication we are confronted with the suffering of the world.

One result has been what some have called "compassion fatigue." I can only feel badly for so many. Then I am exhausted. I shut off and shut down emotionally. I become apathetic. The word "apathetic" means "without passion." To avoid the pain of either my suffering or someone else's suffering, I shut off, I become cool. Emotionally I die. I feel no pain, but also I have shut off my capacity to feel much joy. I find that this describes me and many of my acquaintances. We become clinical. Our society is on a mad search for joy. I suspect we won't find joy until we are willing to face the pain of world hunger, cancer, and the million other sufferings in this fallen universe.

The Response of Denial

The denial of every form of suffering can result in a flight from reality in which contact with the real world becomes thinner and more fragmentary. "It is impossible to remove oneself totally from suffering unless one removes oneself from life itself. . . ." (Soelle, *Suffering,* p. 88).

Denial is one way of dealing with the senseless suffering in life. Escape from life itself. Shut down. Become apathetic. One reason we want to hide from suffering is not only because of its pain but because suffering is a threat to faith in a good God. It seems that we hope against hope that there is a God and that God is good and loving. I know that ultimately I will face the fact of ashes to ashes, dust to dust. When that reality hits, I want to land in the hands of a loving God. Then I look around me and see senseless suffering, and it becomes hard to believe in that loving God. The Psalms are filled with the cries of people in despair. Not all the Psalms sing, "The heavens are telling of the glory of God" (Ps. 19). Some are cries of desperation, "How long, O Lord? Wilt thou forget me forever?" (Ps. 13). "Why art thou so far from helping me, from the words of my groaning? O my God, I cry by day, but thou dost not answer, and by night, but find no rest" (Ps. 22).

Cancer, starvation, earthquakes, all raise a threat to my faith, "If God is good, why this? There must not be a God. If there is, he is not good."

Then I rush around seeking to find some explanation to all the suffering. There are always those who want to explain away suffering. One writer tells of a mother who does not fear for the safety of her sailor son because even if he goes to the bottom of the sea, she says "the bottom of the sea is the hollow of God's hand." That reads nicely in print, but it doesn't wear well when mothers lose their children because of senseless suffering.

The Scriptures record the wrestlings of people with evil and tell of those who try to explain away suffering. Some say suffering is a mystery, but

God has a secret wisdom. Others say God is simply testing us. Still others say God is strengthening us. While yet others explain that God is driving us to our knees and thus to him.

Yes, there may be a mystery to suffering, and God does have a wisdom beyond our sight. Suffering does test us, and for some it does bring strength. Some are driven out of their self-centeredness and into a closer relationship with God. But the danger of all these explanations of suffering is that it leaves the impression that God has somehow caused it all. It says, "God creates children, then creates suffering to test them." That simply is not true. God does not cause suffering. Paul tells us that for those who love God, God can *use* suffering, but we must not conclude from that that God *causes* suffering. Sin and suffering are hostile powers, enemies of God.

The Christian Response

What is the Christian response to the senseless suffering of a fallen and sinful world?

In Romans 8, Paul teaches us to admit the pain we feel ourselves and the pain we feel for others who suffer. He says "we groan." Instead of numbing ourselves and becoming apathetic, or instead of silly human explanations, we need prayers and songs of protest to God and to each other about the pain of the world.

The second thing Christians can do is to act against the suffering. God does not stand by idly and watch the world suffer. Paul says, "What then shall we say to this? If God is for us, who is against us? He who did not spare his own Son, but gave him up for us . . ." (Rom. 8:31-32).

God takes our suffering on himself. He acts to correct the situation. He comes in Jesus Christ not only to suffer with us but to awaken us. If we are the body of Christ, we then must dedicate ourselves to removing suffering in the world. Our task is not only to explain suffering, but to alleviate it. Every person suffering from cancer is a call to himself and to us who suffer with him to do something about cancer. Every child who dies of starvation is a call to the dying and to those who suffer with the dying to rebel against the evils of a fallen world, and to work to feed the hungry.

When we receive the body and blood of Christ in holy communion, we remember that body was given and that blood was shed in pain and suffering not to anesthetize us to the suffering of this world, but to strengthen us to be the body of Christ, and to suffer with, and work toward removing suffering.

When I Face My Own Sin

When I was in third grade my teacher taped my mouth shut with a wide piece of white tape. I was so mortified that I didn't know if I should laugh or cry—although it would have been difficult to do either one—as the other children in the class turned and stared at me, my mouth now finally silent, covered by the tape. I rightly suffered the shame of punishment for disrupting the class. I then had a choice, to grow bitter because of the punishment, or to become better.

Mathematics was never my forte. It still isn't. By the end of the first six-week period of my seventh grade I received an "F," and I was kept after school each night to do extra work. I had a choice when confronted with that punishment; to become bitter and quit, or to become better. I'm thankful that by the end of the term I pulled my grade up to a "B" average.

The evening paper on any day may list items like these:

- Thirty-one-Year-Old Woman Arrested on Credit Card Fraud!

- Local Man Faces Drug Charge!

- Forty-six Fines Levied by the County Court Against Citizens for Reckless Driving

- Minor in Possession of Alcoholic Beverages

These personal incidents and those from the newspaper reflect basic laws of the universe. Break the moral and spiritual laws and you inflict suffering on yourself. Paul reminds us, "There will be tribulation and distress for every human being who does evil . . . but glory and honor and peace for everyone who does good. For God shows no partiality" (Rom. 2:9-11).

Peter reminds us that there are several kinds of suffering. We suffer innocently, we suffer because of our faith, we suffer the just punishment for our sin (1 Peter 2). Much of our suffering we inflict on ourselves. However, being the sinners we are, instead of facing the consequences of our sins, we tend to twist and distort the facts of life to avoid the truth. Morally, we want to be like the man who wants the thrill of a free fall from the top of a high skyscraper, but not the crushing of his body with the "splat" of the sudden stop on the concrete below. Our society promotes free sex without the break-up of family life; self-interest politics, but honest and fair government; a fast buck, but a square deal. The tragedy is that some things simply can not go together. Tonight we examine the suffering God allows us to experience because of our own sins in the hope that we will wake up and return to him.

Deserved Suffering

Three men hang on crosses at the top of Golgotha. Their outward circumstances seem similar. But how different they are in spirit and life. Jesus suffers innocently. Two robbers suffer justly because of their sins.

On one cross is the man who, in the face of his suffering, yields to the impulse to curse and to blame. According to early Christian tradition his name was Gestas. "If you are the Christ, save us!" he barks at Jesus. Salvation for him was the removal of the consequences of his own sin. Salvation seemed to have little to do with forgiveness and becoming at one with self and God. Salvation for Gestas is to do as he pleases and never have to face the music. As we hear his response to his own punishment, it is obvious he has not learned his lesson. He continues to blame. It sounds as if he thinks it is the fault of God or Jesus that he is hanging on a cross.

How blind and twisted is the logic of our sin! Think back to Judas and his dealings with the authorities. It was all right for the authorities to dip into the treasury to bribe Judas to betray Jesus. But when Judas attempted to return the money, suddenly it was "blood money" which the bribing authorities could not accept. Philip Wylie in *Night unto Night* (Part IV) has one of his characters describe this fact of life. "Fifty million or more people in this great and wondrous nation trying as hard as they can to erase all trace of conscience—by one method or another—so that conscience cannot bother them again." Alcoholics Anonymous calls this type of thinking that deludes us from reality "stinking thinking."

Karl Menninger recalls a poem which says,

> "But now I'm happy; I have learned
> The lesson this had taught;
> That everything I do that's wrong
> Is someone else's fault."

(*What Ever Became of Sin,* p. 181)

"One of the criminals who were hanged railed at him, saying, 'Are you not the Christ? Save yourself and us'" (Luke 23:39).

Stinking thinking!

"But the other rebuked him saying, 'Do you not fear God, since you are under the same sentence of condemnation? And we indeed justly; for we are receiving the due reward of our deeds; but this man has done nothing wrong.' And he said, 'Jesus remember me when you come into your kingdom' " (Luke 23:40-42).

A Repentant Sufferer

Dysmas is the name tradition gives to the repentant thief. His sin may have been just as bad as his buddy on the other cross, but his conscience was still alive. I'm sure he did not understand all that Jesus was about, but through the spasms of the pain of his own suffering punishment, he could feel that here was one who radiated forgiveness and care for people regardless of how far out they were, if only they would turn to him. He turns and Jesus answers him, "Truly, I say to you, today you will be with me in Paradise."

Now, I don't know if this is what Jesus meant by those words. But I do know that when you have reached that miracle point where you let God finally break through to you, and you confess your sin, you do hear the word of forgiveness. That is a paradise! The feeling is fantastic.

Both thieves still suffered the same physical consequences of their sin. God does not remove the consequences of our foolishness. Gestas suffered and died alone and unreconciled with himself, with the truth, or with God. Dysmas died in peace.

Playwright T. S. Eliot seems to understand the twisted logic of the Gestas stinking thinking. In his play the *Cocktail Party* these words are spoken, ". . . man is engaged in the endless stuggle to think well of himself." To a psychiatrist one of the characters confesses, "I should really like to think that there is something wrong . . . because if there isn't there *is* something wrong. . . ."

When we sin it seems that we get caught in that futile trap of pretending that the bad is good, that the evil we do is a virtue. It seems that we continue to play that game until either physical or social pain or the pain of inner conscience becomes so great that we are confronted with reality and then repent and start over afresh.

The Johnson Institute for treatment of alcoholism in Minneapolis emphasizes "confrontation therapy." Those who love and care about the alcoholic must confront him, painful and suffering as it is, with the reality of the alcoholic actions. "Very simply, the treatment involves a therapy designed to bring the patient back to reality." (Vernon E. Johnson, *I'll Quit Tomorrow*).

I once spoke with a man whose experience illustrates what we have been talking about. He had been found guilty of a serious crime. He had suffered much agony of conscience, spirit, public shame. So has his family. We spent many hours in counsel and prayer. I asked, "What have you learned from this suffering?"

"If you'd have known me before, you'd know, pastor. I am a different man. I remember the night you first met with my wife and me. I was ready to stop living. Then, after confession and kneeling at the altar in communion, some of the pain began to lift. I know God forgives me. I have come to forgive myself, maybe ninety-five percent. I still have some trouble. But how different I am! For forty years I attended church. It all went in one ear and out the other. Listening without hearing. Now I'm in church every Sunday, twice sometimes. I'm hearing. I'm here because of the comfort and grace. I guess you have to get thirsty before you will drink. Drinking God's word is good for a thirsty man."

Suffering — Truth — Healing

Suffering helps lead us to truth and truth to healing.

Dr. Karl Menninger comments that the experience of repentance brought about by the suffering of conscience and the pain of social judgment can bring us to a state of life that is *better* than before. He suggests that instead of seeking to escape the pain of just suffering, we should realize that the pain is a call to change life and to grow.

"The Prodigal Son's sinful experiences led to a state of existence far better, we are led to believe, than the original one. Mary Magdalene, Peter,

Saul, Paul, St. Augustine were all Prodigal Sons—
sinners indeed—who became 'Weller than well.' "

(Menninger, pp. 185-6)

Harry Emerson Fosdick says of the Prodigal
Son "from the mire of his sin he mined precious
metal." Scripture says of the Prodigal Son, "He
came to himself." We don't know, but I wonder,
if he had not suffered the disgrace of eating with
the pigs would he have found himself?

When our spirits are not at peace and our conscience is paining us, or we are suffering some
punishment, it may do us well to ask, "Is this a
just reward?" If so, then we need to pray for that
sense of guilt which leads us to ask, "Jesus remember me."

Thomas Wilcox in *A Precious Drop of Honey*
gives us good advice, "when the sense of guilt
has been wakened, beware not to try to appease
it by anything else but the blood of Christ or your
heart will become hardened."

A healthy sense of guilt, an awareness of our
sins, leads us to Christ where we can pray, "Jesus,
remember me."

When the Sins of Others Hurt Me

I have seen photographs of a place in which trenching machines dig, one month in advance, the graves of innocent children who die of starvation and medical neglect, while a few miles away the rich romp in their skyscrapers and travel to the beaches in their cars. Why? Because of a consciously designed policy of racial hatred called apartheid. This takes place in South Africa. It is taking place today.

"Behold the Son of man is delivered into the hands of sinners." The innocent suffering at the hands of the guilty is an ancient fact in a contemporary world. In the twentieth century we have simply learned to be more efficient and cold about it. We can do away with millions of dollars through publicly approved policies and few of us are ever the wiser.

"I tell you of one case among others. A young

33

man was arrested by five policemen. They inter-
rogated him, but first he was brought to a torture
chamber. Here he had to strip and then they trod
his body with their shoes . . . he was given electric
shocks on his fingers and toes, and he was bound
. . . and beaten." Later, reports Bishop Auala of
the small black African country of Namibia, he
was found innocent of any charge. This kind of
treatment is not uncommon among the blacks of
this little southwest African country. In 1975 more
than two thousand were literally flogged off their
land and forced to flee. Why? Simply because
they and their church dared to stand for human
rights like food, freedom of speech, the right to
work and to live with one's own family.

"But he was wounded for our transgressions,
he was bruised for our iniquities . . ." (Isa. 53:3).

The innocent suffering at the hands of the
guilty is not new. In the twentieth century we
have simply learned to be more efficient and cold
about it.

YOUNG COUPLE AND TWO CHILDREN
KILLED WHEN DRUNK DRIVER RAMS
BACK END OF AUTO. How many times this
kind of headline has crossed our porch steps and
flashed on our evening screens! An entire family
is wiped out innocently because of the uncon-
trolled drinking habits of someone else.

"I the Lord your God am a jealous God, visiting
the iniquity of the fathers upon the children of

the third and fourth generation of those who hate me . . ." (Exod. 20:4).

John Donne's too often quoted, but seldom heard, phrase summarizes a basic fact of life, "No man is an island, each is part of the main. . . ." In terms of Christian doctrine, we speak of "original sin" meaning not only am I a sinner by nature but also that I live as Isaiah the prophet says, "among a sinful people." We are not free to do our own thing in this world because "our thing" effects the lives of others. We are all part of one spaceship earth, one family of man, afloat on the same piece of matter traveling through space and time. None of us can get off this planet. Thus not a one of us can escape the iniquity, the consequences, the results of the sin of the other. My sin will eventually wash on the shores of someone else. Your sin will eventually hurt an innocent someone else somewhere else.

There have been and will be again more times in your life when you suffer and are hurt, not simply by your own sin, but innocently because of the sin of others. Tonight we focus on suffering because of the sin of others.

The Question "Why?"

Since earliest times people have wondered "Why?" Why do the innocent suffer? One episode of television's "Rich Man, Poor Man" ended with the ashes of an "innocent" man being thrown over the side of a ship at sea. His friend wondered "Why?" I have heard that question asked hundreds of times at the grave-side.

Some answer the question by pointing the finger at the devil. "The devil is the cause of all evil." We use Flip Wilson's flippant comment as he plays Geraldine, "The devil made me do it." In the past few years we have again seen the impulsive exploitation of exorcism and even devil-worship. Evil, Satan, is a power in our lives but never can we "blame" the devil and thereby absolve man. Sin is always an act of man.

Others try to answer the question more piously by saying, "God has sent this suffering" and lay all innocent suffering at the doorstep of God. There is a certain appeal to this kind of thinking which is called "fatalism." Fatalism removes all need to feel responsible for anything in the world. Life and death boil down to luck and "when my number is called." Man becomes a passive puppet in the hands of God. Fatalism is a way of blaming God for everything that happens. "It's the way the mop flops or the cookie crumbles." The real weakness of this attitude in the face of innocent suffering is that God becomes an evil force who plots out trials and temptations for us and there is nothing that we can do about our own lives except somehow endure the consequences. This is not only unbiblical, but not in accord with our expe-

rience of life. God is not the author of all suffering
and I am not helpless.

James says, "Let no one say when he is tempted,
'I am tempted of God'; for God cannot be tempted
with evil and he himself tempts no one; but each
person is tempted when he is lured and enticed
by his own desire. Then desire, when it has con-
ceived, gives birth to sin; and sin when it is full-
grown brings forth death (James 1:13-15).

The Bible makes clear that much of the suffering of the innocent in our world is caused by
the sin of man and is not the will of God. Church
World Service which each year ministers to millions whose lives are torn apart by war and hunger speaks of "Man-made Disasters." "The root
causes of human misery can often be traced to
human selfishness and reluctance to forfeit one's
privileged position for the sake of greater justice
and sharing" (Lutheran World Service Bulletin,
1976).

Remember Isaiah, the prophet who first spoke
most clearly about the suffering of the innocent?
We have taken his words and applied them to
Christ, "But he was wounded for our transgressions, he was bruised for our iniquities" (Isa.
53:5). The focus of those words is not simply on
the fact that someone suffers but *why*—because
of the evil of others. Isaiah rejects the notion that
we suffer because God inflicts suffering on us.
There are times when we suffer simply because

we are all part of one family of man, and when one of us sins we inflict pain on the others. No father can become an alcoholic and hurt just himself. No teenager can commit adultery and hurt just himself. The prop wash of man's sin is felt by the third and fourth generation.

I believe that when I experience innocent suffering, my task is not to get bogged down trying to answer the question "Why?" but rather to ask, "What does God want me to do about it?"

Suffering Transformed

Jesus did not simply accept suffering. He sought God's power to turn suffering into some good purpose. Jesus began his ministry with a focus on those who were hurting. "The spirit of the Lord is upon me, because he has anointed me to preach good news to the poor." Jesus ended his ministry with a vision of the kingdom of God. Those who enter the kingdom will be those who felt the suffering of other men as their own suffering and did something about it. The measure of the Christ-like life will be "the cup of cold water given." Jesus says that everyone who suffers innocently is his brother. Innocent suffering is a call to remove the cause of the suffering!

It is blasphemy for us to sit in church and pray for the hungry and starving of the world if we are not doing anything to reduce the selfishness that feeds on the hunger of the starving. We cannot pray that God will bring justice unless we are doing something to make our community a better place to live.

There are those in the history of Christianity who have tried to glorify suffering as if suffering in itself was good. Suffering, Paul says, produces character. Not always. It depends on what you do with your suffering. If you blame God, or simply silently accept it, suffering can produce bitterness, and can break, rather than build up. For Paul, innocent suffering produced character because he was assured of two things:

First, he did not suffer alone. He knew Jesus as his brother on the cross who also innocently suffered. He knew God was with him and not against him. God was not the author of his suffering.

Second, he knew the will of God was to turn the suffering to a good purpose. So when he was innocently placed in jail, instead of "crying in his beer," he used his situation as an opportunity to convert his jailers.

There are those among us who think we are pious and faithful when we ask, "Why does God permit the Hitlers to kill millions, and millions more to starve to death, and the drunk to run down our children, and the lustful to break up homes?" We know the answer to that!

We are not passive puppets controlled by God. We are his children, free to do *his* will or to do *our* will. God in his love has given us the choice. He has made the consequences of the choice clear. When we choose to do our own thing we injure ourselves and others. When by his grace we choose to do God's will, we bring blessing and peace to ourselves and to others.

God calls the church to be the conscience of the people. The task of the church is to lead a protest movement against all kinds of injustices in our land. Jesus did not idly stand by as the money changers cheated the people at the door-steps of the temple. He took action. He chased them out. If we are the body of Christ we do not simply absorb, absolve, and then explain away the innocent suffering in our world. We are called to rise up in protest. Jesus was not crucified simply because he prayed for the hurting. Jesus was crucified because he helped the hurting.

Martin Luther King summarizes God's Word to us about innocent suffering when the sins of others hurt us: "As my sufferings mounted, I soon realized that there were two ways in which I could respond . . . either to react with bitterness or to seek to transform the suffering into a creative force." He goes on to say, "I have lived these last few years with the conviction that unearned suffering is redemptive. There are those who still find the Cross a stumbling block, others consider it foolishness, but I am more convinced than ever before, that it is the power of God unto social and individual salvation . . . in the midst of the lonely days and dangers I have heard an inner voice saying, 'Lo, I will be with you.' "

(Strength to Love)

When My Faith Is Weak

When I was in seminary I worked for a time as an orderly in a hospital. A young man was critically injured in a motorcycle accident. He was dying. As a result, his wife of several months, who had no faith in anyone or anything beyond herself, collapsed and was hospitalized with an emotional breakdown. The youth's parents, strong devout Christians, led the attending hospital staff in a prayer of thanksgiving for their ministry and the assurance of resurrection to eternal life which their son had in Jesus Christ.

Faith in the Midst of Suffering

I was deeply moved by that demonstration of the difference which faith makes at times of tragedy and suffering. In preparation for tonight's meditation, which focuses on the resources of faith during suffering, I have asked several people from the congregation to share some of their experiences and faith. These are people who have experienced significant pain in life. These are people who have experienced the accentuation of suffering without faith, and the strength that came when they turned to Christ.

One writes, "My words are not very elegant, or intellectually profound. But neither have been my feelings. In the face of our pain my spiritual and emotional life has been at the 'gut-level,' highly intense, filled with basic fears of the possibilities of the unknown. Panic. Disorientation. A tremendous desire to escape from reality by whatever means possible. Constant and continuous anxiety. Emotional outbursts at other family members. A God-how-could-you-do-this-to-us feeling of frustration, hopelessness, despairing. How will we meet the economic realities? The constant pressures. What are the alternatives? Suicide? Booze? These are not the answers."

Another writes, "When hardships or tragedy befall us, our first reaction is to reject every living thing around us, and especially rejection of faith, and then to start to ask 'why?' and to search for faith within ourselves in day-to-day living with the trivial events. You try to shrug off the hurt by going shopping, watching television, getting

drunk or any superficial means to change the pre-
vailing atmosphere. You try most anything when
tragedy first hits. Then you realize it won't go
away by any amount of 'cover-up.' You're alone
in the confused society, searching, asking, beg-
ging, silently screaming for a constant peace or
quiet. You look around and you feel abandoned
by relatives and friends. At times it feels as
though God forgot you. It's not like on television.
There are no Gannons, Welbys, or strong 'magic
men' coming to your rescue. I can't emphasize
enough the loneliness that comes over and takes
hold. All the time you're shaking inside and
searching for something that must be stable, everlasting, and comforting. Of course it's been there
all along, waiting for you to recognize and meet
it—faith the strongest healer and comforter, a
'hand on your shoulder.' "

The father of a family that has experienced
much physical and spiritual pain, comments, ". . .
an answer must be found, it seems. Man? Yes,
man! Doctors. Space-age medicine . . . but oh, not
so. Man is only man, still working on the perime-
ters of human and spiritual knowledge. Man does
not have all the answers. The only balm, logically,
has to be something greater, deeper. Slowly, but
emphatically, the 'realities' are the kingdom and
universe of God where man has, and can, find the
eternal answers to questions.

"Where am I going? I think Jesus struggled; he suffered physical and mortal pain. I have flashbacks from religious, Christian experiences and teachings which gradually, but emphatically, bring me to prayer. The Lord's Prayer for me and the significant passages of the Twenty-third Psalm bring comfort and hope. Many suffer like Christ. By understanding the nature of his burden, we can find hope for eternal relief from these worldly problems. There is no place to turn but to Christ and the hope he has brought to all, including me."

Dr. George Paterson of the University of Iowa Hospital reports that 84% of the parents of handicapped children who were asked about the effect of faith in their lives said it was a significant help (*Helping Your Handicapped Child*, Augsburg, 1975). In light of these personal examples, this kind of study and the witness of scripture, I cannot help wondering how much added suffering we experience because we do not turn in faith to Christ. For the next few moments we will examine three areas of life from the perspective of biblical and personal experience, and the power God gives through faith in Christ.

Faith Frees Me From Myself

Remove my faith in Jesus Christ and what happens to me? I see myself becoming more and more like Peter when he tried to flee from the cross, or like the rich man who wanted salvation but was not willing to give up his many barns full of treasure. Or I see myself like the young lawyer arguing with Jesus about loopholes in the law, worming and squirming to find a way around being the Good Samaritan. Jesus warned us of the results of a lack of faith. "What will it profit you if you gain the whole world and lose yourself?" Without faith I suffer like the Prodigal Son who gained his inheritance but lost himself.

I have the intelligence to know what I ought to do. But of itself my heart will not always choose what I ought to choose. I know that I get locked into myself and my problems, nearsightedness, and self-pity. There are times when I do feel like the paralyzed man who lay at the pool of healing waters for 38 years. I want to get well, I want to change. I want to be more than I am. But I'm frozen where I am. Remember that man? He lay there and watched the healing waters bubble forth 14,000 times and yet he could not bring himself to move to those healing waters. He was stuck where he was. Jesus came to him and asked, "Do you want to be healed?" A foolish question? Of course he wanted to be healed. Did he have the courage to be a whole man? Jesus challenged him. Jesus called forth faith, and commanded, "Rise and walk." He arose and walked. Faith gives us the courage to be what God calls us to be. I like that 11th Chapter of Hebrews, the honor roll of faith.

> By faith Abel offered to God a more ac-
> ceptable sacrifice.
> By faith Abraham obeyed when called
> to go out to a place he did not know.
> By faith the people crossed the Red Sea.

Without faith I am like Peter when he denied Christ, frozen into my lesser self.

Faith Gives Life Meaning

Remove my faith and I have no reason to be. "I think a human being has got to have some faith . . . otherwise his life will be empty. . . . How can you live and not know why the cranes fly, why children are born, why the stars shine in the sky! You must either know why you live, or else . . . nothing matters . . . everything is wild-grass." (Anton Chekhov, *Three Sisters*).

In spite of the suffering Jesus endured, he stood strong. He knew why he lived. He knew why he suffered. "I do nothing on my own authority" (John 5:30), he said. "I came not to be served but to serve." "This is my body and blood given and shed for you for the remission of sins." Faith is the door to understanding. Without it living, suffering, dying are all absurd and empty, like the wildgrass. One line of a pop song goes, "Speak to the sky when things go wrong." The message is similar to our old favorite,

What a friend we have in Jesus,
    All our sins and griefs to bear!
What a privilege to carry
    Everything to God in prayer!
O what peace we often forfeit,
    O what needless pain we bear,
All because we do not carry
    Everything to God in prayer!

Faith, Caring, and Sharing

Without faith, there is no one with whom to share your pain and grief. "Faith is prayer to God, the silent prayer which a man carries in his heart, which he entrusts to God in the hour of need." (Sholem Asch: *A Passage in the Night*.)

When we suffer we need a way to express our suffering. The Psalmist's cry of agony is a physical, psychological, and spiritual necessity, else we are left alone in our pain. Without faith in a God, a God who cares and listens, who is there to turn to? Prayer is as dead as a doornail for many people. If you are on a kidney machine, how much strength can come from a conversation with the machine? If you are suffering cancer, depression, or a broken marriage, try talking to some technological marvel and see how much power you receive.

When I am down I need someone who understands and cares. I don't even need answers so much as a listening heart. I take hope in that brief line from Hebrews that reminds me that because Jesus was a man as well as God, we have a God who is able to sympathize with our weakness. "Let us then, with confidence, draw near to the throne of grace, that we may receive mercy, and find grace to help in time of need" (Heb. 4:16).

Faithlessness is a full cup, so full of my own opinions and strength that I don't need anything more than myself. Faith is an empty cup ready to be filled with the power and presence of God. That is what Paul meant when he said, "I will boast of the things that show my weakness . . . that the power of Christ may rest upon me . . . for when I am weak, then I am strong" (2 Cor. 11:29; 12:9-10).

Jesus knelt in the Garden of Gethsemane. He turned his weakness, his reluctance to suffer, to the Father. "Take this cup from me." Then the turning point of his prayer conversation came, "But thy will be done." The cup of suffering became a cup of strengthening.

Jesus, who knelt in prayer, Jesus the one who suffered, returned to his sleeping disciples clear-eyed and calm. He had it all together. The disciples had the sword-flaying panic. Jesus calmly said, "It is enough; the hour has come. Rise, let us be going."

The disciples scattered and ran into the night. Jesus, through faith, had the courage to be what the Father called him to be. He knew why he lived, suffered, and died. He was not alone. In prayer he and the Father shared each moment.

This is the difference faith makes. St. Paul therefore says, "Examine yourself to see whether you are holding to your faith. Test yourself. Do you realize that Jesus Christ is in you?" (2 Cor. 13:5)

When I Suffer for the Faith

Our children have been blessed because in each congregation we have served they have found older youth who were good examples of Christian young people. Our daughter Kristin has had planted in her mind a very fine model from a former congregation of the kind of person she wants to become. Charles has posted on his bulletin board an article about a young man from this congregation as a good model of what he would like to become.

Each of us has, or at least should have, floating in our mind an example, a model, of what we are striving to become. Oliver Goldsmith said, "People seldom improve when they have no model but themselves to copy." The issue is not whether or not we will have an example or model by which we try to mold our lives, but whether or not that model is worthy of us. The

New Testament is filled with reminders that the ultimate model of life is Jesus Christ. "Have this mind among yourselves which you have in Christ Jesus" (Phil. 2:5).

Take Up Your Cross

Jesus calls us to follow him. "If any man would come after me, let him deny himself and take up his cross and follow me." Jesus, the ultimate example, confronts me not with a model of success, but of suffering. ". . . take up the cross and follow me."

In response to Jesus' call to follow him we have a simple choice: accept or reject, deny self or deny Christ. Scripture gives us an illustration of the choice with two views of Peter. At one point in this disciple's life we see him running from the cross, fleeing from any hint of suffering, scared away from witnessing for Jesus by a little barmaid. Before the night is over he denies three times. Later, Peter has grown spiritually. He stands before the enemies of Christ and is told he must no longer preach or speak about Jesus. Peter boldly replies, "We must obey God rather than men." Peter steps forward, faces the rage of angry men and tells the story of Jesus.

Tertullian, one of the great church fathers, said that he and most of the early converts from paganism were won to Christ not by books or sermons, but by observing how Christians lived or died.

God has given us some examples of how men have accepted the cross of Jesus.

The Martyrdom of Polycarp

One such example of denying self and taking up the cross of Jesus was a man by the name of Polycarp who lived about A.D. 150. Polycarp was one of the last men alive who had known one of the disciples of Jesus. Polycarp was such a strong Christian that he became bishop of the Christian church in Smyrna. Polycarp also became a thorn in the flesh of the Roman government which was promoting worship of the Emperor. Polycarp refused to worship the Emperor. He was taken by soldiers from his home, brought before the governor, and asked to renounce his faith in Jesus Christ. "Eighty-six years I have served him, and he has never done me any wrong. How can I curse my King who has saved me?"

Polycarp was then brought to a Roman arena. The crowd cried for his death. Polycarp was tied to a stake and burned. As he died he prayed, "Lord God almighty, I bless thee because thou hast deemed me worthy of this day and hour to take my part in the number of the martyrs. . . ."

The Example of Kagawa

Eighteen hundred and fifty years later on a Christmas Eve in 1909, a young Japanese man, Toyohiko Kagawa, moved into the slums of Kobe, Japan. He began sharing the love of Christ with people who had been cast out by everyone else. Kagawa knew what it meant to be an outcast. He was kicked out of his home when he decided to become a Christian pastor. Kagawa knew what it was to be homeless. His parents died when he was four years old and he was raised by a drunken brother and then by an uncle. He was graced to meet a missionary who introduced him to Jesus and the first real touches of love. So he was determined to share that love, even if it meant denying himself. At one time sixteen people depended for their bread on Kagawa. He conducted worship services in the slums. Kagawa later became a famous novelist. He spent his profits establishing a night school and then a medical clinic. When Japan made war against the United States, he was arrested because he openly protested the war as wrong and selfish. His neighbors called him a traitor. "Kill Kagawa, the Traitor" posters appeared all over the city.

Kagawa knew what Jesus meant when he told his disciples, "If the world hates you, know that it has hated me before it hated you. If you were of the world, the world would love you . . . if

they persecuted me, they will persecute you . . . "
(John 15:18ff).

From Polycarp in A.D. 155 to Kagawa in the
twentieth century, the common element in the
lives of these men is the cross of Jesus. They both
denied themselves and willingly suffered for the
sake of someone else, because that is what Jesus
did.

Not All Suffering Is Christian

Not all suffering is Christian suffering. How
many times we piously utter the cliche, "I guess
that is my cross to bear." Sometimes what we
are referring to is our arthritis, or a stingy rela-
tive, an irritable boss, the fate of being born in
the wrong place at the wrong time. Such suffering is not cross-bearing for Jesus. At other times
our suffering is the result of our own sin. Peter
makes it clear that not all suffering is the suffering
of the faithful. Sometimes it is because of our
foolishness (1 Peter 2:21).

Cross-bearing is to voluntarily "take upon
ourselves" the sin and hurts of another. Jesus
volunteered, not army style with no choice, for
the cross. Time and again he makes it clear he
did not have to go to Jerusalem. He could have
avoided the cross. "But for our sake he who was
rich became poor so that we might become
rich" (2 Cor. 8:9).

Simon of Cyrene who carried the cross for Jesus part way up the Via Dolorosa is not held before us as an example of Christian suffering, for he had no choice. Simon did not step forward and volunteer to reduce the pain of the weight of the cross on a hot and dusty day. He was *"seized"* and the cross was laid on him.

Christian suffering is a *willingness* to volunteer for duty to help someone else have a chance to live a more human life, and in the process we face the hurt and rejection of those who couldn't care less.

Bearing the Cross Today

It is difficult to understand how to take up the cross of Jesus in our super-complicated twentieth century where one-third of the world gives lip service to the virtues of Christianity, but pays real homage to the gods of selfishness and nationalism.

In the days of persecution under the Roman empire and even today where persecution of the Christian is practiced, it is rather clear how to give witness. You can take up the cross by being a Christian martyr. In yet another day, the medieval ages, one witnessed for Christ, took up his cross, by rejecting the world and running off to hide in the monasteries, escaping the "evil world."

But how do we "take up the cross" today? There are few who will openly persecute us for confessing Christ. It has almost become the new religious fashion to speak about your faith. If anything, Christian talk is on the verge of becoming cheap. However, running off and hiding in the mountains in a personal monastery and leaving the world behind to stew in its own juices is hardly a means of witnessing for Christ, hardly a sacrifice. A place in the mountains where I can occasionally hide and rest would be a pleasure and not at all suffering for Christ. A monastery might be rather pleasant.

Dietrich Bonhoeffer speaks of it this way, "When Christ calls a man, he bids him come and die. It may be a death like that of the first disciples, or of Luther *leaving* a monastery." His point is that following Christ is leaving a former way of life behind. It is death to that on which you are hooked and keeps you from sharing yourself with others. On what are you hooked? What in your life is the drag that holds you back from "taking up my cross"?

Taking up the cross may not bring persecution and martyrdom, nor is it necessarily rejecting the worldly places in which we live. Instead, I suspect it is daring to thrust ourselves into the politics of our own community and denying ourselves some pleasure of escape into the security of our own little private religious and family worlds, in order to bring healing of the mind to the confused, through better mental health, and feeding the hungry through better farming and economics and politics.

If our Christianity has ceased to be serious about personal involvement in the community for Christ, our religion has then become a watered-down private, emotional jag. "Christianity without discipleship is always Christianity without Christ." (Dietrich Bonhoeffer, *Cost of Discipleship*, p. 50.) Therein is the cross today, "Involvement in the world for Christ's sake."

Where besides in your home and personal life are you bearing the cross? Wherever it might be, Jesus our Brother is with you!

When My "I" Gets in the Way

On a recent flight I was assigned the uncomfortable middle seat. Squeezed in between two other passengers, each of whom kept my ears busy with conversation, the talk turned to the state of world affairs. "Isn't it awful about all those people killed in the Middle East?" exclaimed the woman to my right. "You'd think after all these years the Arabs, Jews, and Christians would tire of fighting," commented the man to my left. "Well, how about the Irish Catholics and Protestants, bombing and killing each other, all in the name of Christianity!" replied the woman on my right. "It's a good thing the world isn't any more religious than it is."

That was the final comment of the conversation. An uneasy silence cut through the constant chatter. My mind echoed the last comment, "It is a good thing the world isn't any more religious

than it is." I wanted to argue that point. It isn't
the *religions;* it's the ego-centeredness of the
people who *claim* to be religious that cause the
problem. Not one of these religions teach war
and hate. But the damage had already been done
by the selfishness of the members of each of the
religions referred to.

To Bring a Blessing

When Jesus entered Jerusalem for the last
time, the crowd chanted, "Blessed is he who
comes in the name of the Lord! Peace in heaven
and glory in the highest." Jesus and we, his
people, are to bring a blessing and not a curse
to the world; peace to man and not hatred and
prejudice and war. In the liturgy for holy communion we sing, "Therefore with Angels and
Archangels and with all the company of heaven
we laud and magnify thy glorious name; ever
more praising thee. . . ."

"Laud and magnify thy glorious name" that
is our task. Yet there are some of us who in the
name of religion spread hate and prejudice and
build walls instead of bridges between people.
Ghandi, the great leader of India, was once asked
why he was not a Christian, since he so lived the
Gospel of Jesus' love. His reply was like that of
the man on the plane, "I'm not a Christian be-

cause I have met too many Christians." A comment like that is devastating!

"Blessed is he who comes in the name of the Lord. . . ." That is our call to bring and share the blessings of Christ. It is one thing to wave the banners and slogans of the faith and sing loud praises to the name of Jesus. That makes our egos feel good. But it is another thing to carry the cross, absorb suffering, and bring the blessing of peace.

I believe we are called to be echoes of God's love down the corridor of time, the hands and feet of Christ, his body on earth to bring a blessing and not a curse. But there are times when my "I" gets in the way of Christ. I then become a curse rather than a blessing.

Through the Bible the Lord charges us: "I the Lord your God am holy; you my people are to be holy." Jesus says, "Come follow me." "I have set you an example to follow" and he kneels down and washes the feet of his disciples. St. Paul summarizes what we are called to be, "Have this mind among yourselves which you have in Christ Jesus, who though he was in the form of God did not count equality with God a thing to be grasped, but emptied himself, taking the form of the servant, being born in the likeness of men. And being found in human form he humbled himself and became obedient unto death."

Pride vs. Humility

To conform our lives to the image of Christ, to magnify and laud his glorious name, that is our calling. Yet, how unnatural it is. I would rather puff myself up with false pride rather than show true humility. The call to be a Christian goes one hundred eighty degrees counter to my natural instincts. I am tuned to magnifying *my name,* not yours or God's. We hire public relation firms, NBC spends hundreds of thousands on a new logo. We rent billboards and have protocol so no one is socially slighted. We print a long list of letters before and after our names to protect our titles. There is a built-in insidious desire to tear down another, and we silently smile in the secret places of the heart over the fall and failures of others in hopes it will advance us, magnify our own name above all others. Rather than to release the innocent, there is in the heart of man a desire for vengeance, scapegoats to carry the blame. We cry "release Barabbas and crucify, crucify."

So Pilate gave sentence . . . and Jesus died on the cross. How unnatural it is to magnify someone else's name—unless that someone else and I are bound together as one. That is why St. Paul, when Christ is born in him and he devotes his life to living for Jesus says, "It is no longer I who live but Christ who lives within me." Before I can magnify the name of Christ, and become a blessing to you, he must be in me and I must become at one with him.

The presence of Christ makes a difference in the way we live. It transforms us from banner-waving ego-boasting "Christians" to cross-bearing children of God. Lloyd C. Douglas, in his novel *The Robe* tells of young Marcellus who converted to Christ during his stay in Palestine. He came back home to Rome and talked with Diana, his girl friend who did not approve of his new faith. She replies, "What I feared was that it might somehow affect your life—and mine, too. It is a beautiful story (this story of Jesus). Let it remain so, we don't have to do anything about it, do we? Let us plan to live, each for the other, just as if this hadn't happened." Marcellus was silent. Then he said, "But it has affected my life. I couldn't go back to living as I did, even if I tried. I couldn't."

Thought, Word, and Deed

How can we magnify and laud Christ's name? How can I become a blessing so that instead of people saying, "It is a good thing the world is not more religious," they will say, "Blessed is he who comes in the name of the Lord."

The first way is in "thought." We sin in thought, word, and deed. Thus the reverse, magnification of God's name, must be in thought, word, and deed. St. Paul says in at least three places in scripture that the mind, the thoughts, are essential to what we are. "Have this mind among yourselves which you have in Christ Jesus." "Be renewed in your minds." "Think on these things which are true, lovely, good. . . ."

Second, our words bring either a blessing or a curse to our neighbors and world. A letter in one of Ann Landers' columns says it well, "The most vicious killer of all time is not disease, it is gossip. Gossip destroys friendships, causes anxiety, humiliation, heartbreak, and more trouble than any single thing I know of."

Our words are powerful. They can kill or give life. A medical doctor went through his training as an agnostic. After completing his work in a Christian college, going on to medical school and becoming a successful physician, one day he became a Christian. He returned to visit his old campus and told the president, "All that time I was asking questions and acting as a skeptic—which I was—what I really was looking for was not an answer to all my questions. I was looking for some professor who would dare to stand and say, 'Jesus Christ is real to me.'" Magnify the Lord in thought, word, and deed.

An employer had two applicants for work in front of him. He noticed that both applicants carried recommendations from their ministers.

Shrewdly the employer looked at them and said, "You know we don't work on Sundays. Haven't you a reference from someone who sees you on week days?" There are times when we find it too easy to speak of our Christian faith with words and those words begin to ring hollow unless that is what we are as persons. If it were not for the fact that what Jesus teaches is true, I'd hesitate to ever preach, because I know my words for Christ come much easier than my deeds.

Magnify God's name in thought, word, and deed. Christ offers himself and his grace to us today. His call enables us to be holy, to be pure, to magnify his name, to abstain from the evil and to do the good. "Be ye perfect as my heavenly father. . . ." But this is not all he offers you.

Someone told a reformed alcoholic, "I see you have mastered the devil at last." "No," came his quiet answer, "but I do have the Master of the devil."

Jesus offers you himself. "This is my body and blood given and shed for the forgiveness of your sins." Christ comes humbly—not in glory but on a cross. Christ comes not just for perfect followers but for sinners and failures. He forgives us and promises to be with us. "I will not leave you alone. I will be with you always." If you will take him in, he is willing to be in you so that you can magnify him in thought, word, and deed.

HOLY

WEEK

SERMONS

Jesus—The Suffering Lamb

> Sometimes I think upon the Cross
> And close my eyes and try to see
> The cruel nails, crown of thorns and
> Jesus crucified for me.

"Behold, the lamb of God who takes away the sin of the world!" Few words have struck so deeply into the human mind and spirit, and have stayed for so long as the poetic and revealing words John the Baptizer spoke when he saw Jesus coming toward him. Jesus came walking out into the wilderness, down the bank to the water's edge at the river Jordan. He came humbly, accepting the sin of the world. He who is the Son of God, asking to be baptized by John as if he bore the very same guilt and sin as the rest of us. Jesus' baptism was his acceptance of the job, the task God had given him. Jesus' baptism by the prophet John was his acceptance of all the sin and guilt of the world though he, sinless, needed no baptism.

"Behold the lamb of God who takes away the sin of the world." Few words describe the life of Christ as well as these. These words are part of our worship language preserved in the Gloria in Excelsis and the Agnus Dei sung by Christians around the world.

Behold . . .

John begins "behold." "Behold" means more than "look" at Jesus, "see" Jesus. John must have been terribly moved by the spirit when he, the first man to recognize Jesus as the Savior, uttered these words. We would best understand the word "behold" to mean "heads up," "awake," "stir up the flames of faith in your heart," standing with us is the Son of God. More deeply "behold" means "receive" into your life, hold Jesus in wonder and awe, drop everything else, come a-running, accept Jesus as your savior. "Behold" is a call to faith.

Lowell Mason, the hymn writer, interprets the word "Behold" in the hymn

My faith looks up to thee
Thou Lamb of Calvary, Savior divine!
Now hear me while I pray,
Take all my guilt away,
O let me from this day be wholly thine.

Behold the Lamb

Behold the "Lamb." Jesus is not only our shepheld who is with us in the valleys of the shadows of death. He is the Lamb. He is the one who by his innocence, and quiet, meek, humble service sneaks up on death and destroys it in the resurrection. In Jesus' day the word "lamb" meant one who was innocent, gentle, pure. In Exodus, the twelfth chapter, the Lord instructs the people to put the blood of an innocent lamb on the doorpost as a sign of their faith and obedience. Then the angel of death will pass over them. Christ is our "passover lamb." By his pure obedience he gives us the promise of everlasting life, that the angel of eternal death will not destroy us forever. In the Old Testament a lamb is a sacrifice, the "scapegoat" that bore the punishment of the guilty. In place of the guilty going to the gallows, the lamb was sacrificed on the altar. So John says the Lamb "takes away the sin of the world."

Five hundred years before Jesus, the writer of the fifty-third chapter of Isaiah described the kind of person our Savior would be.

He was despised and rejected of men.
A man of sorrows, and acquainted with grief;
He was despised and we esteemed him not.
Surely he has borne our griefs and carried our sorrows.

He was wounded for our transgressions,
He was bruised for our iniquities;
Upon him was the chastisement that made us
    whole.

All we like sheep have gone astray.
We have turned everyone to his own way;
And the Lord has laid on him, the iniquity of
    us all.
He was oppressed, and he was afflicted, yet
    he opened not his mouth,
Like a lamb that is led to the slaughter . . .

Behold the LAMB!
    Hear the Negro spiritual that describes the
lamb . . .

They put on Him a thorny crown
And he never said a mumblin' word.
They put on Him a thorny crown
My Lord, He never said a mumblin' word.

They nailed Him to the cross,
And he never said a mumblin' word,
They nailed Him to the cross,
My Lord, He never said a mumblin' word.

See how they done my Lord;
He bowed His head and died.
And He never said a mumblin' word.
My Lord, He never said a mumblin' word.

Action Words

"Behold" "lamb," "who takes away the sin of the world." "Take away." Notice how not a word in the Bible tells us how Jesus looked, the kind of clothes he wore, the color of his hair, the size of his bank account or in what kind of a neighborhood he lived! The Bible uses verbs, action words to describe Jesus. We are prone to describe people by the neighborhood in which they live, the car they drive, the clothes they wear. But listen to how Jesus is remembered and described. Listen to the action words:

> "Takes away sin"
> "Healed many"
> "Raised from the dead"
> "Had compassion"
> "Fed the people"
> "Wept"
> "Rejoiced"
> "Laid hands on and blessed"
> "All your sins will be forgiven"
> "Taught them many things in parables"
> "Ate with sinners"
> "Prayed"
> "Suffered"
> "Rose from the dead"

Action words describe the lamb who takes away our sins. Where do the verbs, the works of Christ stop? He "did," "gave," "acted," in any task. None was too lowly, too disagreeable, too frustrating— even to the point of touching the ugly, wretched leper and the beggar. Jesus didn't do a lot of big talking about kindness, being merciful and forgiving rather than judging. He was big in deeds of kindness, mercy, service. He had compassion. Because of him we know that God is love.

Take Away the Sin of the World

If there is any lesson or admonition for us here, it is the verb "take." "Take away the sin of the world." We must not just think about forgiveness and mercy. We must *be* forgiveness and mercy. Only the act, the actual deed of your forgiving rather than judging, being compassionate rather than bitter, serving rather than being served, can remove the sin that holds you off and away from others and Christ.

"Behold the lamb that takes away the sin of the world." In the book of Revelation it says that those of faith are washed clean in the blood of the lamb. God no longer counts it against those of us who believe . . . who "behold" the Lamb.

There is only one way to remove sin. That is to carry it away and bury it. Removing sin is like washing dirt out of clothes. Some agent must penetrate the cloth and pick up the dirt and carry it away. It is the person Jesus Christ who seeks to penetrate your life and take away your guilt and sin, to wash you clean.

When we are confronted with a sinful brother, we have a choice. We can get rid of the sin by getting rid of the sinner. We can reject him, cast him out, destroy him; or we can get rid of the sin by accepting the sinner, enduring the pain, the hurt, the sharp words, the anger, thus taking away the sin by absorbing it. We, too, are called to be "lambs," to penetrate the sinners whom we face, and carry away their sin, and so let Christ, through us, redeem them.

It is not the conqueror, the manipulator, the political "guessers" who in the end have exerted the greatest power over the human race. It is the "lambs," those who have moved others by self-denying, mercy, and love and have exerted on our history, the silent pressure of faith and hope.

> Under an Eastern sky,
> Amid a rabble cry
> A man went forth to die
>   For me!
>
> Thorn-crowned His blessed head,
> Blood-stained His every tread,
> Cross-laden on He sped,
>   For me!
>
> Thus thou was made all mine
> Lord make *me* wholly thine,

Give grace and strength divine
To me.

In thought and word and deed,
Thy will to do; oh! lead my feet
E'en though they bleed
To thee.

"Behold the lamb of God who takes away the
sin of the world!"

Let us pray: O Christ, thou Lamb of God, that
takest away the sin of the world,
have mercy upon us. O Christ, thou
Lamb of God, that takest away
the sin of the world, Grant us thy
peace.

Amen.

Jesus Cries from the Cross

"My God."

— a curse, "My God!"

— an exclamation of surprise, "My God?!"

— a prayer in anguish, "My God, help."

— a shout of faith, "My God!"

Hanging from the cross Jesus' thick and dry tongue formed the opening words from the 22nd Psalm. "My God, my God, why hast thou forsaken me?" In his last hours of life Jesus hangs onto and runs through the words of the 22nd Psalm. The words are not a curse, nor a cry of resignation in the face of death, but the conversation of a lonely man in the agony of death by torture. While we know the 23rd Psalm by heart, Jesus must have known this psalm just one step away. He gives us a glimpse into his mind and heart as he hangs on the cross.

> "Why art thou so far from helping me,
> from the words of my groaning?
> O my God, I cry by day, but thou dost
> not answer; and by night, but find no
> rest."

The cross was not a pretty scene. It was no stained glass cross, no eighteen-karat gold cross backed by soft music and light. It was a painful cross, a bitter, cursing scene, mingling blood and sweat and an untimely end. Death. A hammer was raised toward the heavens and all at once it came crashing down. Nerves go numb for minutes as spikes twelve inches long split each tender hand and foot and a guiltless man is driven to the cross. Then the hanging. The nerves are no longer numb, but raw.

My God, Why?

"My God, my God, why hast thou forsaken me?" Jesus has not given up faith. The Father is still his Father but now he knows the agony of despair unto death. "Where are you God? Where is the justice in all this?" He flings his "Why?" into the face of the Father. "Why? My God, I have done my best. I have given all I have to do right. I have healed the sick. I have preached to

the poor. I have fed the hungry. I have befriended
the friendless. I have spent myself until I had
nothing, no home, no place to lay my head for
rest."

Most of us at one time or another have wondered where the justice of it all is. When we have
broken our backs to do right, when we have done
our best and the best wasn't what people wanted,
when we have sacrificed something of ourselves
and the sacrifice was ignored and rejected—most
of us have experienced something of this some-
time. Now magnify that kind of feeling by the
cross and you may have a glimpse into the heart
of Jesus.

"But I am a worm, and no man;
  scorned by men, and despised by the
    people.
  All who see me mock at me,
  they make mouths at me, they wag
    their heads;
  'He committed his cause to the Lord;
  let him deliver him.' "

The soldiers strip him and cast dice for his
clothes. His mother and a couple of friends are
left. But that is all!

Jesus is experiencing hell! His physical agony
is magnified by the agony of being a social outcast, and the agony of the spirit. What is left for
him? His friends either betrayed him or fled him

to save their skins. He has given all he has to give but that wasn't good enough, or at least what the crowds wanted. Jesus has no dignity as a human being left. He feels like a worm, not a man. Even his faith is made fun of. What is left? Hell.

"What is hell? Hell is oneself, Hell is alone, ..."   (T. S. Eliot, *"The Cocktail Party"* (Act I)

Alone

No man has ever been so much alone. Despised, rejected, forsaken, tried, in the throes of death denied. "Alone!" is the cry of the Crucified.

"My God, my God, why hast thou forsaken me?"

Jesus looks up and what does he see but his enemies circled around him like bulls in a bull ring, he feels like a lamb with a broken leg and the lion open-mouthed roaring down on him to tear him bit by bit.

Jesus tries to hold on for a few moments longer. He remembers back to the days of childhood and how he knew God's love then through his mother, a loving touch on a tired head, a bandage on a wounded knee, a warm meal at the end of a tiring day. But now, he is tired unto death. There is no strength left. "My strength is dried up, my tongue sticks in my mouth" (vv. 14-15).

Hell. Jesus is experiencing hell. John Calvin interprets "Descended into hell" to mean just what

Jesus experiences—the pain, the hatred of innocent suffering because of our sin. It wasn't, he insisted, a trip to a geographical location. It is descriptive of Jesus' experience when our sins were laid on him.

Sin always separates. Sin always isolates and leaves us alone. Sin builds walls between us and others, between us and God. Jesus now hangs on the cross and experiences that pain of our sin—alone.

In Bremen, Germany, there is a granite crucifix, and under it the words are engraved: "Sinner, See Thy Work!"

What is going through Jesus' mind these last minutes on the cross? He looks on the hatred of man in the face, and we are like mad dogs on the attack.

> "Yea, dogs are round about me;
>   a company of evildoers encircle me;
>   they have pierced my hands and feet—
>   I can count all my bones—
>   they stare and gloat over me;
>   they divide my garments among them,
>   and for my raiment they cast lots."

A contemporary song gives the feeling of that moment: "All the lights went out in heaven . . . except" the song says, except in the broken heart of God the Father. This is what Jesus, too, experiences. His "My God, my God," is a cry of a man in the agony of hell, of rejection by everyone, but there is yet a thin thread of life with God, a small stream in the desert of the soul. Jesus still cries "*My* God." At the moment all is dark. But he still trusts. At the end of the psalm he sings silently in his spirit, "He, God, has not despised the affliction of the afflicted, He has not hid his face . . . he has heard when he cried . . . the afflicted shall be satisfied; those who seek him shall praise the Lord."

Resurrection Hope

There is hidden in the cross the light of the resurrection, just as there is hidden at the end of this psalm of suffering the faint light of faith in a just and merciful God. Jesus knows that though he die; his death was not without purpose. Jesus knows, as he cries, "My God!" that his suffering is not useless. Jesus knows that someone somewhere will see the cross, hear his cry, and the hard shell around their lives will be cracked open and the seed of love and faith in God will find a place. For some of us that is what it takes, the stark shock of tragedy to crack us open to God.

Hidden at the end of the psalm is the prayer, "May your hearts live forever!"

The dogs have done their worst. He begins to cry, "My God!" He finishes praying, "May your hearts live forever!"

Jesus Our Brother Overcomes

When I conducted my first funeral service in a little Pennsylvania mountain town I was so nervous, I could not remember the Lord's Prayer. Since then I have been the pastor at many funerals, and I have attended the funeral of my father and dear members of our family. Neither time nor experience, not even depth of faith has removed the nervousness, the awe, the starkness of death. I think of the numbness that overcomes me and those to whom I minister at the hospital or in private homes when a loved one dies. We cry a little, mumble a few words, and repeat the story of the disease, accident, or death. We make a few plans. We hold hands. We pray the Lord's Prayer.

There is a sting to death that is not removed this side of eternity. Early in life you court a girl or boy. You hold hands, fall in love, marry, bring up children. You pray and play together. Then illness or tragedy closes in. You hold hands, perhaps in the hospital. Then there is that moment. You are no longer holding hands. One of you is gone. Dead. Not here.

The message of Easter is addressed particularly to you who this past year or years have stood or are standing at the edge of the grave. In our congregation alone we have been to the grave thirty-two times since last Easter. The promise of Easter is especially for you.

Overcoming Failure

Couples come to my office bewildered, confused when they discover that their marriage is empty, dying. Usually just one of the marriage partners comes first. There are tears. There is hurt. There is emptiness at home. One has left or is emotionally gone. There is guilt and shame and a sense of failure. A marriage that began with high hopes, flowers, and dreams has decayed into hopelessness, weeds, nightmare. We try to put things back together again. Sometimes we can. Sometimes we can't. Marriages die and fall like people. God has a message for you who have shared in this kind of death.

Easter is for those of us who have stood at the shores of failure, and have the courage to admit we are not all that we pretend to be, that we are not all the great successful businessmen that

Success Unlimited or the *Power of Positive Thinking* says we ought to be.

Easter is God's message for sinners, for those of us who have let hatred capture our tongues and hearts, selfishness rule our pocketbooks, lower choices make our decisions.

The Offer of Hope

Easter is God's Word to the dying and grieving, the broken-hearted, the failures and sinners. I suspect by now I have listed most of us. For those of us who, somewhere along the path of living, have discovered that we need God, we need a power, a hope beyond ourselves, we especially are prepared to hear God's promise in Easter. Someone has said, "You don't know what hope is, until you have lost it. You only know what it is not to have hope."

So to you who are troubled, Jesus says, "Let not your hearts be troubled. You believe in God, believe also in me. In my Father's house are many mansions; if it were not so, I would have told you. I go to prepare a place for you."

That is the Easter promise. "Even though you die, yet shall you live." That is his promise.

"Rise, your sins are forgiven." That is an Easter gift.

"Lo, I am with you always." That is his eternal promise to you.

I share with you a note I received this year from a parishioner whose life was opened by her difficulties, and she received anew the promise of Christ:

> "A miracle has happened! After fighting for nearly twenty years not to cry, I am now able to cry and it is such a relief. I am so grateful to realize that I can't cope with all my problems alone and that I am not as self-sufficient as I thought I should be. God is reaching me. I am letting go. I hope never to feel that I have to be so self-sufficient again."

The Gift of New Life

On that first Easter the women were on their way to the tomb. Pilate had thought he had secured the grave of Jesus against all possibilities. He had a large gravestone rolled in front of the door and guards placed outside. As the women made their way, they worried, "Who shall roll away the stone, for it is heavy." To their amazement God had rolled away the stone. What they could not do, God did. To their amazement Jesus was not dead, but alive. What man can not do, live forever, God gives us. New life!

There was no tomb tight enough, no grave secure enough, no hole deep enough to keep

Christ buried. Christ promises to you, "There is no death, no failure, no sin so strong that can defeat you." In Christ, you have the promise of forgiveness and resurrection to life everlasting.

Now, I don't understand that! I don't understand how Jesus can be crucified, dead, and buried, and then a gravestone rolled away and he be raised from the dead. But then, there are many things I don't understand. I don't understand the love of my wife for me. She could have married a richer, wiser, kinder, more handsome man. I don't understand how the kernel of seed corn mixes with earth and water and sun and becomes a giant food-producing plant. What I know of truth and life is like the little boy at the beach. He brings his sand bucket filled with water from the ocean to his father and says, "Daddy, here is the ocean!" To which his father chuckles, "Yes, son, but there is a lot more where that came from." I may understand some truths, but there are many more that I can't get into the bucket of my mind.

But Easter does not depend on my understanding. "We reside," says Dr. Weatherhead, "in a suburb called time. We inhabit a lodging in space called earth, a little speck of temporary matter floating about the universe. . . ." How can I possibly understand Easter and eternity? The promise, "You who live and believe in me even though you die" does not depend on my mind. It depends only on what St. Paul declares, "But in fact, Christ has been raised from the dead."

There are a lot of wrong, rotten, and unjust things in our world. There are a lot of people who, in the face of sin, death, failure and broken hearts, simply become bitter. But as Maxwell Anderson (in *Key Largo*/Prologue) says, "I have to believe there's something in the world that isn't evil. I have to believe there's something in the world that would rather die than accept injustice, something positive for good that can't be killed, or I'll die inside."

We too need someone beyond ourselves. Easter brings us the promise of the Risen Christ, the Christ who has overcome all! Easter symbolizes his promise that in him we too shall overcome!

Resources for Worship from Augsburg

Augsburg Sermons

The Church Year Calendar and Lectionary prepared by the Inter-Lutheran Commission on Worship has enjoyed a popular and enthusiastic acceptance. It has met a real need. So has **Augsburg Sermons**—a series of preaching resources based on this Calendar and Lectionary. Each volume in this series contains a sermon for every Sunday in the Church Year plus all the major festivals. Volumes now available are:

Gospels—Series A (Matthew) 280 pages
Gospels—Series B (Mark) 272 pages
Gospels—Series C (Luke) 288 pages
Epistles—Series C 288 pages

For the Children—
The Gospel for Children
Object Messages from the Gospel of Mark
by Harold J. Uhl

Simple objects like a map, a flag, and a camera catch the listener's attention and illustrate the point of these 60 messages based on the Gospel of Mark. The specific texts are the same as those in **Augsburg Sermons** — Gospels — Series B and therefore fit naturally into the Sunday worship services. Teachers and parents will find that these messages are also ideal for church school classes or for family devotions.
128 pages. Paper.

Good News From Luke
Visual Messages for Children
by Lavern Franzen

These visual messages are intended to focus a portion of the worship service especially toward children. Not only do they accomplish this, but are popular with adults also. The messages in this book follow the Gospel texts in **Augsburg Sermons**—Series C, but they can also be used independently of worship services—for family devotions, in the classroom, and also for senior citizens.

128 pages. Paper.

Other books of Gospel messages by Lavern Franzen for children to see and hear are:

SMILE! GOD LOVES YOU 128 pages. Paper.

SMILE! JESUS IS LORD 112 pages. Paper.

Prayers for Today's Church
edited by Dick Williams

"To pick this book up in the morning, or at night, or any time, and to browse through its pages, is to be led into a world where we meet the hopes and fears of the human family, the deep stirrings of our own hearts, and the limitless mercies of God."

From the Foreword by Alvin N. Rogness

Here is a collection of nearly 500 prayers that express the concerns and aspirations of our present time. The prayers are arranged in three categories:

I. Prayers for Christmas, Easter, Pentecost, and other church festivals.

II. Prayers of intercession which give voice to a vast array of human needs, hopes, and longings.

III. Prayers for special occasions such as preparation for Holy Communion, anniversaries, and other special moments in one's spiritual life.
216 pages. Paper.

The Psalms in Christian Worship
A Practical Guide
by Massey H. Shepherd, Jr.

The revival of interest in the use of the Psalms —in new translations and musical settings—is one of the notable signs of renewal in contemporary worship. Creative innovation in such renewal, however, can only be effective if it is rooted in a sound knowledge of worship tradition. This book offers that knowledge.

This practical guide will help pastors and church musicians to plan and use the Psalms effectively in the liturgical services of the church and in the private devotion of its members.
128 pages. Paper.

Counseling Resources for the Pastor
Make Your Illness Count
by Vernon J. Bittner

A hospital chaplain shows how God's healing power can be released in your life.

Chaplain Bittner shares his experiences with patients facing the crisis of illness. He has found that illness can be a destructive experience—even if you get well. But it doesn't have to be. In this book he shows how you can make your illness a constructive experience—an experience you can learn from.

Chaplain Bittner shares many real life illustrations of what happens when God's healing power touches a person's life. Most important is the realization that for many people illness can bring with it the unexpected rewards of emotional and spiritual growth.

128 pages. Paper.

When Going to Pieces Holds You Together
by William A. Miller

You can find healing when you allow yourself to grieve.

This book deals with the experience of personal loss: the death of a loved one—major surgery — financial disaster — divorce. These are some of the things that can shatter your world—that can make you "go to pieces."

Chaplain Miller points out that this "going to pieces" at the time of loss is a normal and natural human experience. Furthermore, it might be the very thing that will "hold you together" as you work through the grief process.
128 pages. Paper.

Who's Running Your Life?
by Marge and Erling Wold

You can gain control of your life and make it more productive and satisfying.

Living a full life, the life that God intended for us, does not happen by chance. But we all have the potential for realizing this fullness of life. Marge and Erling Wold show us how to unlock that potential so that with God's help we might reach our goal of personal happiness.
128 pages. Paper.

No More for the Road
One Man's Journey from Chemical Dependency to Freedom
by Duane Mehl

Clergyman, seminary professor, responsible husband and father, Duane Mehl began using barbiturates to ease the pain in his back. This was the first step on the long road to chemical addiction. He takes more and more pills to deaden pain and to induce sleep. Then he adds alcohol as the need for pills increases. He fights addiction and struggles to maintain respectability.

Friends commend him for being so joyful in the face of pain; actually he is "stoned" most of the time. Finally he hits bottom and can't go on.

Mehl enters a treatment center. He recounts his treatment, his painful return to his colleagues and family, and how he found freedom through the resources of his faith.

This book debunks some myths and stereotypes about chemical addiction, gives strong warnings about drug abuse, including alcohol, and provides practical advice for families facing chemical dependency.

144 pages. Paper.

What to Do When You're Depressed
A Christian Psychoanalyst Helps You Understand and Overcome Your Depression
by George A. Benson

Dr. Benson helps us to understand why certain things depress us; he helps us to understand the problems of others; in short, he helps us to understand ourselves. And this is the key to overcoming depression.

Dr. Benson combines the insights of psychoanalysis and the resources of the Christian faith with its assurance that God identifies with us, forgives our guilt, and nourishes us in the hope of life with him now and forever. 144 pages. Paper.